Favorite HOUSEPLANTS
A GROWER'S POCKET GUIDE

DIANE MOREY SITTON

ILLUSTRATIONS BY
WAYNE F. MICHAUD

GIBBS·SMITH
P
PUBLISHER

SALT LAKE CITY

CHECKLIST FOR SUCCESS

A vigorous indoor garden begins with healthy plants. Shop carefully, following these guidelines.

1. Choose houseplants with luster. Reject specimens that have dropped their lower leaves or that have dull, lifeless foliage.

2. Inspect plants for evidence of insects or diseases. Examine the stems and both the tops and bottoms of the leaves. Signs to look for include holes, punctures, and leaking.

3. Check the foliage for dry, brown tips and edges. These symptoms may be signs of water stress.

4. Select full, bushy plants instead of plants with leggy, elongated stems.

5. Flowering plants in full bloom have lost much of their splendor. For longer-lasting beauty at home, select plants whose buds are just ready to unfurl.

6. Check the surface of the soil and the drainage holes in the bottom of the pot. If roots show in either place, the plant may be rootbound. Select another.

7. Help houseplants adjust to their new home by placing them in cool positions out of direct sunlight for one week. Check the water daily. As a safeguard against pests and diseases, quarantine the new plant for two weeks.

GREEN THUMB BASICS

Houseplants bring a world of greenery indoors. To maintain their beautiful foliage, brilliant flowers, and enticing fragrances, you must understand and meet their basic needs.

SHOWERING THEM WITH LIGHT

All plants require light, although they differ in the amount of light they need. Generally, plants receiving too little light become leggy and develop a tendency to drop their leaves. Plants receiving too much light wilt and become faded or scorched. Plants are usually more tolerant of a light deficit than an excess.

It is the nature of plants to turn their leaves toward the light source. Occasionally rotating plants positioned near windows helps them to maintain pleasingly balanced shapes.

Artificial light, supplied by fluorescent tubes, makes it possible to grow plants in low-light areas. Regulate these "grow lights" with automatic timers to provide twelve to sixteen hours of illumination a day.

QUENCHING THEIR THIRST

How much water a plant requires depends on the variety of plant and the conditions surrounding it. A plant grown in a clay pot requires more frequent watering than an identical specimen grown in a plastic container. Likewise, a plant grown in potting mix amended with perlite or sand requires daily checking, while a plant with its roots sunk in humus-rich potting soil may only need to be watered once a week. Light, temperature, humidity, season, and the size and placement of the container affect the watering schedule as well.

Following a rigid regimen may lead to overwatering or underwatering. Instead, learn the plant's requirements, and check the soil before watering.

The simplest way to test moisture is to push your finger an inch into the soil. If it feels damp under the surface, you may decide to withhold water for another day.

Applying water directly onto the top of the soil is one of three commonly used techniques for watering houseplants. Using this method, water thoroughly until water seeps out the drainage holes in the bottom of the pot.

If thick, overhanging foliage or other conditions make it impractical to water from above, set the pot in a shallow pan containing an inch of water. Add more water if needed. Remove the pot when the surface of the potting soil feels damp. Let any excess water drain before returning the plant to its permanent location.

Submerging pots in water up to their rims replenishes moisture in potting soil that has been allowed to dry out completely. Two signs indicate this serious condition: potting soil that has shrunk away from the sides of the pot and water that runs freely from the top of the soil out the bottom of the pot during watering. Lift the pot from the water when air stops bubbling to the surface.

Plants appreciate tepid water; cold water shocks tender foliage and roots. In areas with hard water, pamper indoor plants with frequent drinks of distilled water. In pollution-free regions, spoil them with rainwater.

Most houseplants adapt to normal room temperatures ranging from 65 to 75 degrees Fahrenheit with a nighttime drop of 5 to 10 degrees. Many suffer stress if temperatures fluctuate more than 20 degrees within a 24-hour period. To ensure healthy plants, avoid positioning them near heating units, air conditioning ducts, or other locations with strong air currents. In winter, avoid placing plants near doors where they are subjected to sudden, chilling drafts.

Nearly all houseplants require humidity levels of fifty percent or higher. Signs of inadequate moisture in the air include shriveled or scorched foliage and dry or browning leaf tips. Spraying a fine mist of water is an immediate, but temporary, method to increase the level of moisture around indoor plants. Sitting potted specimens on trays of moist pebbles is another simple way of providing humidity. Another technique calls for double potting; that is, placing one pot within another and then packing the space between the two with dampened peat moss.

SATISFYING THEIR APPETITES

As houseplants develop, producing new foliage and flowers, they gradually deplete the nutrients in the confines of their pots. Feeding plants with fertilizer containing equal portions of nitrogen, phosphorus, and potassium ensures balanced growth.

Generally, nitrogen benefits foliage and stems, phosphorus builds a strong root system, and potassium ensures sturdiness. Manufacturers market other fertilizers for specific purposes or groups of plants.

SINKING THEIR ROOTS

Commercially prepared all-purpose potting soil meets the needs of most houseplants. It is easy to amend. Lighten it by adding perlite or vermiculite; enrich it by incorporating organic amendments such as leaf mold or peat moss.

Specialized mixes meet the needs of specific families of plants. For instance, African violet mix is high in humus to accommodate the needs of this acid-loving family. It is recommended for begonias and philodendron, as well. Cactus mix, a gritty, well-drained formula matter, meets the needs of cacti and many succulents.

ASPARAGUS FERN

Asparagus sprengeri

With its billowy, soft green foliage and cascading stems, asparagus fern conjures up images of Victorian parlors. And rightly so. This easy-to-care-for South American native has been a favorite of indoor gardeners for generations.

Emerald fern, as it is sometimes called, gets its feathery appearance from tiny, flat needles that cover its two-foot-long stems. It is not a true fern but a relative of garden asparagus.

Grow asparagus fern in hanging baskets where its cascading foliage is showered in bright, indirect light. It thrives in all-purpose potting soil kept uniformly moist. Propagate the plant by root division. Divide established plants every three years. Feed it sparingly, and protect it from extreme cold.

DONKEY'S TAIL

Sedum Morganianum

Few succulents adapt as well to hanging baskets as donkey's tail, an unusual plant with long, drooping stems. Not only do the thick, fleshy leaves overlap in an armorlike fashion, but they are covered with whitish dust, called bloom. One look at the plant and it is easy to see why other common names include burro's tail and lamb's tail.

This Mexican native is a good candidate for sunny corners where the foliage will not be disturbed. The small leaves fall off easily if brushed against. If a mishap occurs, insert the bottom of the leaf into sand to propagate a new plant.

Grow donkey's tail in equal parts potting soil and sharp sand. Let the surface of the soil become dry to the touch between waterings. Occasionally, donkey's tail surprises growers with small pink flowers at the ends of stems, but it does not flower readily. This succulent does not require feeding.

IVY GERANIUM

Pelargonium peltatum

Trailing stems with shiny ivy-shaped leaves and clusters of showy flowers in shades of salmon, pink, lavender, rose, and red make ivy geranium an asset to any indoor decor. The flowers, most abundant in spring, are often veined with a darker hue of the dominant color.

Grow this South African native in hanging containers positioned by sunny windows. It prefers a cool, dry environment with well-drained potting soil. Allow the surface of the soil to dry to the touch between waterings.

Ivy geranium blooms more profusely in small pots than large ones. Feed this heavy bloomer with liquid fertilizer. Propagate it by cuttings in spring or fall. Groom the plants by removing wilted flowers and foliage.

PURPLE PASSION VINE

Gynura sarmentosa

Both the long, twining stems and the dark green leaves of this beauty are cloaked with purple, velvety down, giving the plant an air of grandeur and earning it another common name, "royal velvet plant."

Grow this regal beauty in hanging baskets near sunny windows where the light will enhance its color. Give it all-purpose potting soil and moderate amounts of water, allowing the surface of the soil to dry to the touch between waterings. Avoid wetting the velvety foliage. Purple passion vine produces orange flowers in spring or summer. Removal of the unpleasantly scented discs encourages the development of new, richly colored growth. Contain this fast grower and promote fullness by pinching off long stems. Start new plants from cuttings. Feed it once a month.

SPIDER PLANT

Chlorophytum comosum

Few plants are as engaging as spider plant, an easy-to-grow ornamental species enjoyed by indoor gardeners since Goethe, a German writer, brought it into his study nearly two hundred years ago. Besides its strikingly variegated, arching leaves, "ribbon plant," as it is also called, sends out long, pale yellow stems that bear small, white flowers followed by miniature plants.

Although this South African native withstands a variety of growing conditions, it does best with bright light, ample water, and all-purpose potting soil. Feed the plant every two weeks.

Remove the plantlets for propagation or leave them on the stems of the mother plant to create a cascading appearance.

SWEDISH IVY

Plectranthus australis

Although this easy-to-grow beauty is known as Swedish ivy, it is not from Sweden, and it is not an ivy. It originally hails from warm climes, including the temperate regions of Australia, and it is a mint. The name evolved because of its popularity in Sweden as a plant for hanging baskets.

Although Swedish ivy has squarish stems, aromatic foliage, and spikes of small flowers characteristic of the mint family, it is the plant's round, waxy, scalloped leaves and trailing nature that earn it a place in indoor gardens.

Give this fast grower bright, indirect light and all-purpose potting soil kept evenly moist. Nip off long stems that develop on mature plants to encourage full growth. Stem cuttings root easily in soil or water. Regular feedings encourage large, lush foliage.

AFRICAN VIOLET

Saintpaulia species

Who doesn't remember a grandmother or favorite aunt with a collection of African violets that lined her windowsills or graced a lace-covered tabletop? Since collectors discovered them in Africa in the late 1800s, these blooming beauties have won the devotion of indoor gardeners.

As in Victorian nosegays, soft, velvety leaves in low rosettes surround clusters of single or double blooms in white, blue, purple, pink, or red. Flower petals can be splashed, dotted, or edged with contrasting hues.

The secrets of success with African violets include ample light but no direct sun; consistently moist soil; warm, consistent temperatures; high humidity; and regular feeding. Grow *saintpaulia* in African violet mix. Avoid exposing the plant to direct sunlight. Create new plants by rooting individual leaves.

BIRD OF PARADISE

Strelitzia reginae

The bloom of this exotic, flowering plant invokes images of lush, tropical settings. Not only is the boatlike bract plumed with orange-and-purple flowers that give it the appearance of an exotic bird, but it perches on top of a slender, green stalk above a fan of dark green foliage.

In the wild, this South African native grows into a large plant; in indoor gardens, crane lily, as it is sometimes called, grows three to four feet tall.

Place this flamboyant bloomer where its tropical foliage can luxuriate in direct sunlight for part of each day. Plant young specimens in eight- to ten-inch pots filled with all-purpose potting soil kept evenly moist. Feed it with liquid fertilizer during the growing season. Repot it when necessary, using the opportunity to separate rooted sections for propagation.

CHRISTMAS CACTUS

Schlumbergera 'Bridgesii'

The trumpeted, red flowers that decorate this jungle cactus during the holiday season are only one of its assets. The remainder of the year, Christmas cactus decorates its surroundings with its unusual, arched branches made up of flat, bright green segments.

In its native South America, members of this species grow in trees, where they sink their roots in moist pockets of leaf debris. To simulate a jungle habitat, place Christmas cactus in bright, indirect light, avoiding full sun. Use a porous potting mix, such as African violet mix, or equal parts all-purpose potting soil and peat. Keep the soil evenly moist. Fertilize weekly except immediately after blooming.

The short days of fall stimulate holiday flowering. For timely blooms, put the plant in the dark at sunset.

KALANCHOE

Kalanchoe blossfeldiana

There is nothing timid about this 'Flaming Katy.' It enlivens sunny windows with splashes of scarlet flowers, sometimes numbering fifty per cluster. The color and duration of bloom make it one of the most popular succulents for indoor gardens.

Like other members of the succulent family, kalanchoe has thick, fleshy foliage. The attractive, shiny leaves are tinged with red along their scalloped edges.

Grow kalanchoe in all-purpose potting soil loosened with coarse sand. Let the surface of the soil become dry to the touch between waterings. Reduce water after the blooms fade. Fertilize sparingly.

Kalanchoe naturally blooms in spring, coaxed into flowering by the short days of winter. Forms with orange, yellow, or apricot flowers are available. Propagate by leaf cuttings, stem cuttings, or seed.

WAX BEGONIA

Begonia semperflorens–cultorum

The attractiveness of their white, red, and pink flowers in single, semidouble, or double forms and their ever-blooming nature make wax begonia a colorful addition to the indoor garden.

Their versatility makes them popular as well. Their easy-blooming habit, waxy, round leaves, and colorful foliage are equally attractive tumbling over the rims of hanging baskets or filling windowsills with cheerful color.

Grow these fibrous, rooted begonias in African violet mix or other well-drained potting soil. Water when the surface of the soil is dry to the touch. Avoid overwatering. Feed wax begonia with liquid fertilizer every two to three weeks. Start new plants from stem cuttings.

BIRD'S NEST FERN

Asplenium nidus

This stately fern has shiny, apple-green fronds that unfurl from its fibrous, brown core. The resulting bowl-shaped rosette accounts for the plant's common name, bird's nest fern. Although the slender fronds can grow four feet long in tropical outdoor settings, indoor specimens rarely exceed two feet.

Like most of its relatives, bird's nest fern appreciates a warm environment, indirect light, well-drained soil kept evenly moist, frequent mistings, and occasional feedings. It relishes rainwater, especially in areas with hard water from the tap. New plants are started from spores produced on the undersides of the foliage.

With minimal care, this long-lived beauty can decorate indoor environments for many years.

COLEUS

Coleus blumei

The word "color" is synonymous with coleus, for few plants exhibit a richer palette than this tropical shrub. The velvety leaves are splashed with yellow, red, green, orange, and purple in double or triple combinations. The leaves themselves can be heart-shaped or oval with scalloped or ruffled edges.

Flame nettle, as it is also called, is a fast-growing member of the mint family. With bright light, a warm environment, all-purpose potting soil kept evenly moist, and regular feedings, young plants grow to two feet tall in one season.

Nipping flowers and pinching stems encourages full growth. Coleus is easy to propagate from stem cuttings taken in spring or summer.

CROTON

Codiaeum variegatum pictum

Few shrubs can compare with croton when it comes to bold, show-stopping color. Not only is the foliage splashed, striped, banded, veined, and spotted with bold hues of yellow, green, red, orange, copper, pink, brown, and ivory, but in some crotons the colors of young leaves differ from the colors of mature leaves.

The shapes of the leaves are as varied as their colors. Although all share a waxy texture, foliage may be long and narrow or short and wide. Configurations include lobbed, ribbed, crinkled, and corkscrew.

Direct sunlight enriches croton's leaf color. Other essentials include a draft-free, warm environment and all-purpose potting soil kept evenly moist. Provide moisture by placing the pot on humidifying trays. Propagate croton by stem cuttings taken in spring or summer. Feed regularly.

DUMB CANE

Dieffenbachia maculata

This comely evergreen adds a tropical ambience to indoor settings with its ivory and green mottled leaves that spiral outward from the trunk. But beware of the sap. If touched to the tongue, it causes temporary speechlessness and pain, hence the common name, dumb cane. The plant is also known as mother-in-law's tongue.

When its needs are met, dieffenbachia thrives indoors, attaining heights of up to five feet. Position the plant in a bright spot. It benefits from warmth, high humidity, and misting. Use all-purpose potting soil, allowing the surface of the soil to become dry to the touch between waterings. Fertilize moderately. Wash your hands after removing faded leaves or taking cuttings for propagation.

REX BEGONIA

Begonia rex–cultorum hybrids

The ongoing fascination with rex begonia began in 1856 when a plant collector in England unboxed an orchid. There, in the pot, grew a *B. rex–cultorum*.

Today, rex begonia is the most commonly grown foliage begonia. And no wonder. The large, roughly textured leaves are patterned in silver, pink, maroon, red, green, and lavender.

King begonia, as it is also called, thrives in bright light and warm, humid environments. Pot it in all-purpose potting soil. Small containers accommodate its shallow roots. It cannot tolerate wet feet, so allow the soil to become dry to the touch between waterings. Fertilize it regularly. Propagate it by stem or leaf cuttings.

Miniature forms of *rex begonia* are an ideal size for windowsill gardens.

WATERMELON PEPEROMIA

Peperomia argyreia

Whether displayed on a table, shelf, or windowsill, watermelon peperomia is packed with pizzazz. The appeal begins with the plant's red stems and continues to the pointed tips of the satiny, heart-shaped foliage emblazoned with stripes of silver and green. To some, the markings resemble watermelons; hence the common name.

Like other members of this decorative family, watermelon peperomia produces long, white, pencil-thin flower spikes. It grows best in bright light, warmth, and a humid environment. Give it all-purpose potting soil supplemented with peat moss. Water when the surface of the soil feels dry to the touch. Avoid overwatering, and feed sparingly.

Small pots accommodate the plant's root system. Propagate it by tip cuttings taken in spring or early summer.

CALAMONDIN ORANGE

Citrus mitis

Not only is calamondin orange the most popular indoor citrus, decorating sunny breakfast nooks and bright patios with its glossy foliage and four-foot stature, but it rewards growers with edible fruit.

The small oranges, borne at the tips of the branches, turn from green to bright orange through a three-month ripening process. Ripe fruit may be harvested or left on the tree for several months.

To ensure a year-round crop, position calamondin orange in a sunny location. Plant it in all-purpose potting soil, allowing the surface of the soil to become dry to the touch between waterings. Provide nutrients regularly with tomato-type fertilizer. Calamondin orange is easy to grow from seeds.

FIDDLE-LEAF FIG

Ficus lyrata

Its size and fast-growing nature make this one of the most commanding container plants. Specimens, which grow in single-stalk fashion, reach five feet or more and carry leaves fifteen inches long and nine inches wide. The huge, dark green, violin-shaped foliage not only characterizes *Ficus lyrata*, but accounts for its common name, fiddle-leaf fig.

Like many members of this large, tropical family, fiddle-leaf fig likes warmth, medium to bright light, and all-purpose potting soil allowed to become dry to the touch between waterings. For consistent growth, give the plant frequent, light feedings, and protect it from sudden changes in the environment. Drafts or other stress cause leaf loss.

Keep the plant looking fresh by cleaning the leaves with a moist cloth. Propagate it by air layering.

PARLOR PALM

Chamaedorea elegans

With its arching, light green fronds and clusters of small, yellow fruit that occasionally develop, parlor palm adds a tropical flair to any indoor setting, whether it's a living room, breakfast nook, or screened patio.

Like many members of this large family, "good luck palm" is a slow grower with a neat, predictable form. Its fronds consist of narrow leaflets arranged in pairs. It reaches three feet tall.

Meet its easy-to-care-for needs by giving it moderate temperatures, bright light, all-purpose potting soil kept evenly moist, and occasional mistings. Feed it sparingly, and groom it by removing old growth. Do not prune parlor palm.

SCHEFFLERA

Brassaia actinophylla

This impressive plant is esteemed for its glossy, green foliage that radiates outward from the tips of the stems like the sections of an umbrella. The striking configuration of the leaflets accounts for several common names, including Queensland umbrella tree, octopus tree, and starleaf.

Besides its magnificent stature (plants grow to six feet or more), schefflera is valued for its fast-growing, long-lived nature.

Warmth, lots of bright light, and all-purpose potting soil satisfy this easy-to-grow plant. Allow the surface of the soil to become dry to the touch between waterings. Fertilize sparingly. A large container provides room for growth. Occasionally bathe the foliage with a damp cloth.

MONSTERA

Monstera deliciosa

In Southern Mexico and Guatemala, this jungle vine travels up tree trunks by means of its aerial roots. The enormous, heart-shaped leaves are deeply cut and perforated in unusual patterns. They account for the common names Swiss cheese plant and hurricane plant.

In indoor environments, provide a moss or bark-covered support for this imposing grower. When its basic needs are met, monstera reaches the ceiling and spreads up to eight feet wide.

Although monstera is tolerant of a wide range of conditions, it prefers warmth, bright light, and all-purpose potting soil. Allow the surface of the soil to dry to the touch between waterings. Direct the aerial roots into the soil or onto supports. Feed it regularly, and sponge the massive leaves to keep them clean. Propagate it by stem cuttings.

CAST IRON PLANT

Aspidistra elatior

Cast iron plant acquired its common name during the Victorian era because of its ability to survive in dimly lit parlors filled with heat and vapors from gas lights. The dark green, leathery leaves of this robust plant stand upright from the rootstock on six-inch-long stems. Modest, deep purple flowers form around the base of the plant.

Although this slow-growing, long-lived plant tolerates neglect, it thrives if given medium light and all-purpose potting soil allowed to become dry to the touch between waterings. More problems develop from overwatering than underwatering. It cannot tolerate boggy soil.

Cast iron plant appreciates regular feeding during spring and summer. Propagate it by plant division in spring.

CHINESE EVERGREEN

Aglaonema commutatum

The most notable characteristics of this robust plant are the glossy, lance-shaped, dark green leaves splashed with silvery gray markings and the creamy white flowers followed by clusters of reddish berries. However, it is the plant's ability to tolerate neglect that makes it a favorite with indoor gardeners.

Although Chinese evergreen withstands poor light and dry air, it prefers medium light and humid environments. Pot it in all-purpose potting soil kept evenly moist. In dry environments, place the pots on saucers filled with moist pebbles. Propagate it by stem cuttings or plant division. Chinese evergreen will grow in water. It benefits from monthly feeding.

HEART-LEAF PHILODENDRON

Philodendron oxycardium

The trailing stems of this popular houseplant can be encouraged up supports or allowed to spill from pots or hanging baskets. Either way, the dark green, glossy, heart-shaped foliage adds a luxuriant touch to indoor settings.

Originally from the steamy jungles of South America, sweetheart plant, as it is sometimes called, is a strong, robust grower conditioned to shady environments. Although it withstands neglect, it prefers average temperatures, bright light, and African violet mix or all-purpose potting soil amended with an equal proportion of peat moss. Keep the soil barely moist.

Feed it regularly, and pinch out the tips of the stems to encourage fullness. Clean the leaves to enhance their glossy surfaces. Propagate it by stem cuttings.

PEACE LILY

Spathiphyllum species

When the exotic blooms of this plant first appear, they are white as doves, which explains the common name, peace lily. Soon the color changes to light green and remains so for the five- to six-week duration of each bloom. Flowers of peace lily form at the ends of long, slender stalks above lush, dark green foliage that mimics the shape of the blooms. *Spathiphyllum* 'Mauna Loa' grows to two feet tall. Flower stalks can reach twenty inches long.

Although spathe flower, as it is sometimes called, tolerates dry, shady conditions, it appreciates care. Place this easy-to-grow favorite in bright light where its lush foliage can soak up humidity. Encourage healthy growth with all-purpose potting soil amended with peat moss and kept evenly moist.

Maintain the plant's vigor with regular feedings. Clean the foliage occasionally with a damp cloth. Propagate it by plant division in spring.

POTHOS

Epipremnum aureum

Its perky appearance and versatility make this climbing plant a common choice for indoor gardens. Fill a container with water and let the shiny, heart-shaped leaves of golden pothos decorate a windowsill in the kitchen or bathroom with their green-and-yellow variegation. Grow it in an indoor planter, or pot it in a small hanging basket. Grow it up a slab of bark, or train it along a wire. The type 'Marble Queen' has creamy white foliage flecked with green.

Although devil's ivy, as it is also called, can endure excessive heat and poor light, it prefers normal room temperatures, bright light, and all-purpose potting soil kept evenly moist. Snip out the growing tips to increase fullness. Propagate it by stem cuttings rooted in soil or water. If the variegation fades, move pothos to a brighter location.